PIONEERS IN HEALTH AND MEDICINE

The Life of

Charles Drew

PIONEERS IN HEALTH AND MEDICINE

The Life of

Charles Drew

Katherine S. Talmadge

Illustrated by Antonio Castro

Twenty-First Century Books

A Division of Henry Holt and Co., Inc.

Frederick, Maryland

Published by
Twenty-First Century Books
A Division of Henry Holt and Co., Inc.
38 South Market Street
Frederick, Maryland 21701

Printed in Mexico

10 9 8 7 6 5 4 3 2 1

Library of Congress Cataloging in Publication Data
Talmadge, Katherine S.
The Life of Charles Drew
Illustrated by Antonio Castro

(A Pioneers in Health and Medicine Book)

Includes index and bibliographical references.

Summary: A biography of the black surgeon who was
noted for his research on blood plasma.

1. Drew, Charles Richard, 1904-1950—Juvenile literature.
2. Surgeons—United States—Biography—Juvenile literature.
3. Afro-American surgeons—United States—Biography—
Juvenile literature. [1. Drew, Charles Richard, 1904-1950.
2. Physicians. 3. Afro-Americans—Biography.]

I. Castro, Antonio, 1941— ill. II. Title. III. Series: Pioneers in
Health and Medicine.

RD27.35.D74T35 1991 617'.092—dc20 [B] 91-29854 CIP AC
ISBN 0-941477-65-7

Contents

Chipping Away
7

Foggy Bottom Boyhood
15

"Big Red"
24

Dr. Charles Drew
34

Blood Pioneer
44

Time of War
53

A Tough Teacher
64

A Handful of Years
75

For Further Reading
83

Index
84

1

Chipping Away

Charles Drew just couldn't sit still—not when he was this nervous. The hours dragged by as Charlie and his wife, Lenore, waited for the telephone to ring. It was a December day in 1948, and Charles Drew was worried about "his boys."

Charlie's "boys" were his former students, young doctors he taught at the Howard University Medical School. Drew had trained these men to be among the first African-American surgeons. He was known as a severe teacher, one who set the highest standards for his students.

On this winter day, those standards were being tested. Several of the young men Charles Drew had trained were at The Johns Hopkins University. They were taking an examination given by the American Board of Surgery. If they passed the test, they would be certified by the board as surgeons, joining a small group of medical pioneers.

In 1948, there were about 180,000 doctors in the United States, but only 4,000 of them were black. Only 92 black doctors had received advanced certification in their medical fields.

Seven years earlier, Charles Drew himself had been one of the first African-American doctors to be certified as a surgeon. Since then, he had dedicated his career to teaching. One of his colleagues, Dr. Paul B. Cornely, noted that "the training of young Negro surgeons" was Drew's "all-consuming" interest. "He wanted to train Negro surgeons who would meet the most rigid standards," Cornely observed.

"The boys whom we are now helping to train," Drew once wrote, "in time will constitute my greatest contribution to medicine."

So Charles Drew waited anxiously for some word about his "boys." Lenore Drew recalled how her husband responded to the day's events:

> *Some people talk things out when they're worried. Not Charlie. He went down to the basement and, with a sledgehammer, began knocking to pieces an enormous old coal bin that had been cluttering up the place for years.*
>
> *"Your boys will do all right," I tried to console him.*
>
> *"All right won't be good enough," he said. "They're up there at Hopkins competing with*

graduates of the top medical schools—with rich boys, Lenore, boys who've had every advantage."

I went back upstairs. An hour passed, and the booming of his hammer grew louder. Finally, the phone rang.

"That was President Mordecai Johnson over at Howard calling," I told Charlie. "He's heard from Hopkins, and he said to tell you one of your boys taking the examination came in second."

"Second!" Charlie threw down his hammer and let out a whoop.

"But that's not all," I went on. "He said to tell you another one of your boys came in first!"

Charlie dropped into a chair. "First," he said unbelievingly. "First out of all those students from all over?" Tears filled his eyes—they had already filled mine—and his voice dropped to a whisper. "First and second. Well, what do you know about that?"

The outstanding performance of Drew's students that day was only the beginning. By 1950, eight of his students had been certified by the American Board of Surgery. That was more than half the number of black surgeons certified between 1941 and 1950.

Charles Drew was a pioneer in the education of African-American medical students. His work greatly increased the opportunities available to black doctors.

In the process, the quality of medical treatment for Americans of all races was improved. Charles Drew considered teaching to be his most important work and his most lasting legacy, but his contributions to medicine and public welfare did not end there.

Charles Drew was an accomplished surgeon. He was the first African-American doctor to receive the degree of Doctor of Science in Medicine, a prestigious degree that few doctors achieve. And Drew was the first black surgeon to be appointed as an examiner for the American Board of Surgery.

Drew was also prominent in medical research. By the time he began to teach at Howard University, he was already well known for his contributions to blood research. Drew was a leading figure in the development of safe methods for blood transfusions. He discovered new ways that blood could be collected from donors, preserved, and safely given to people who are injured or sick.

Other scientists had experimented with different ways of storing, or "banking," human blood. But it was Drew who succeeded in bringing together these threads of scientific research. He designed the procedures that are still used in blood banks today. And he did so at a time when there was a desperate need for banked blood: the year 1940, when the world was deeply embroiled in World War II.

On June 12, 1940, in response to England's critical needs, American relief agencies began the "Blood for Britain" program. For the position of assistant director, the Red Cross selected a doctor and scientist who had already established himself as an expert in blood banking. They chose Charles Richard Drew.

During that fall and winter, under Drew's careful supervision, tens of thousands of units of blood were collected from American donors, and then processed, preserved, and transported to Britain. The British not only received life-saving shipments, they also learned Drew's system of blood collection and processing. In months, the British were creating their own supplies.

The success of Drew's "Blood for Britain" effort led the U.S. government to start a massive collection program in preparation for its involvement in World War II. Once again, Drew was chosen to supervise a national blood collection program. His work would eventually lead to the establishment of blood banks in every major medical facility in the world.

This is the story of a dedicated teacher, a talented surgeon, and a tireless researcher. It is also the story of a man who devoted his energies to the fight for civil rights. On that day in 1948, when Charles Drew demolished an old coal bin with a sledgehammer, he was trying to destroy something larger. He was trying to break down a wall built by racial prejudice.

As a young man, Drew had come up against that wall many times. Growing up in Washington, D.C., going to school at Amherst College, and training to be a doctor at Canada's McGill University—throughout his early years, Drew suffered from the disappointments and indignities of racial prejudice. Even as a leader of America's blood drive during World War II, Drew felt what he called "the sense of continuously being an outsider."

This sense of being an outsider is what caused Drew to see his teaching as more important than anything else. For he wanted to teach more than surgical techniques. Charles Drew tried to give his students, in his words, "the greatest type of moral courage":

The thing which we have not had in the past is a group bound by similar training, aspirations, and ideals to which we could feel that we belonged. The sense of belonging is of extraordinary importance to men as individuals and as groups. The sense of continuously being an outsider requires the greatest type of moral courage to overcome before actual accomplishments can be begun. Our fellows are rapidly creating something which gives them a sense of "belonging to." Within the protection of this feeling, they should be able to accomplish more than the fellows who have gone before.

All his life, Charles Drew faced the wall of racism that separated white and black in America. If he could have, Drew would have taken a sledgehammer and knocked it to pieces.

That wall, as Drew knew only too well, had been cluttering up the place for years. Racism was "a high-walled prison," he wrote:

> *There are so many things still unknown in almost every realm of knowledge, and the need for this knowledge is so great that any new addition not only is accepted, but the individual who creates the work is accepted without very much regard to race, color, or creed.*
>
> *There are many difficulties to overcome, it is true, but our greatest difficulty still remains in the fact that . . . so much of our energy is spent in overcoming the constricting environment in which we live that little energy is left for creating new ideas or things.*
>
> *Whenever, however, one breaks out of this rather high-walled prison of the "Negro problem" by virtue of some worthwhile contribution, not only is he himself allowed more freedom, but part of the wall crumbles. And so it should be the aim of every student in science to knock down at least one or two bricks of that wall by virtue of his own accomplishment.*

Charles Drew spent his life chipping away at the wall built by racism. His achievements served as a model for the young men and women who followed him. His story is a record of courage and conviction— the record of a medical pioneer and an advocate for social change.

2

Foggy Bottom Boyhood

Nestled near the banks of the Potomac River in Washington, D.C., there is an area known as Foggy Bottom. The neighborhood was named for the thick clouds of fog that often roll in from the river in the early morning and evening.

Charles Richard Drew was born in a large, old house in Foggy Bottom, on June 3, 1904. He was the first child of Nora and Richard Drew. They named their son after his uncle Charles, and they called him by the nickname "Charlie."

Foggy Bottom was a middle-class neighborhood, home to many families with Irish, Italian, French, or African roots. It was a pleasant place for a child to grow up. There was the nearby river for fishing and swimming; there were plenty of yards and vacant lots for baseball games; there was a park across the street; and there were many neighborhood kids, both black and white.

Although people of different races lived together there as neighbors, the Foggy Bottom area was not integrated in the true sense of the word. There were two swimming pools in the park—one for blacks and one for whites. There were four elementary schools—two for blacks and two for whites.

The Foggy Bottom community was typical of the times. Racial segregation was widespread, a legacy of the days of slavery.

The U.S. Census of 1860, taken the year before the Civil War began, showed that there were four million blacks living in the United States. Ninety percent of them were slaves. Many were Africans who had been transported by slave traders to America, where they were purchased by plantation owners. The children and grandchildren of slaves were born into slavery.

Slaves were not allowed to vote or own property. Frequently, they were not even permitted to learn to read and write. Married slaves had no guarantee that they would be allowed to stay together or see their children grow up, and many families, in fact, were split up by their "owners."

On January 1, 1863, almost halfway through the Civil War, the first step in the long struggle for equal rights occurred when the Emancipation Proclamation went into effect. The proclamation freed those slaves who lived in states fighting against the Union.

Most slaves did not become free until the Civil War ended in 1865, when the U.S. Congress adopted the Thirteenth Amendment to the Constitution, which outlawed slavery. In 1868, Congress passed the Fourteenth Amendment, which guaranteed former slaves equal treatment under the law. The Fifteenth Amendment, passed in 1870, made it illegal for any state to deny, on the basis of race, the right to vote.

But freedom according to the law did not result in freedom or equality according to people's attitudes. Despite federal laws that insured equal rights, blacks continued to face the inequities that were imposed by racial prejudice.

In the years following the Civil War, some states attempted to weaken the constitutional amendments designed to enforce civil rights. For instance, southern states enacted various laws to deprive black citizens of the right to vote.

Many states also passed laws to separate blacks and whites. These laws, called "Jim Crow" laws after a character in a folk song, created separate facilities for blacks and whites. Racial segregation was the rule at public facilities such as schools, playgrounds, bus stations, and swimming areas. Private facilities, such as restaurants and hotels, were also separated by race. It was even common to see drinking fountains with signs that read, "For Whites Only."

Segregation by race gained a national footing in 1896. In that year, the U.S. Supreme Court decided, in a case called *Plessy v. Ferguson*, that blacks could be forced to use separate facilities from whites as long as those facilities were equal. This idea became known as "separate but equal."

In fact, the public and private facilities set aside for blacks were almost always inferior. In effect, then, when the Supreme Court accepted the basic idea of "separate but equal," it actually allowed separate and *unequal* treatment on the basis of race.

When Charles Richard Drew was growing up in Washington, D.C., Jim Crow laws, and the attitudes that they were based on, put daily restrictions on his life. It was widely accepted that black children would go only to "black" schools and swim only in "black" swimming pools. But such restrictions did not keep the Drews and their black neighbors from establishing a strong sense of community.

The Nineteenth Street Baptist Church helped to promote that sense of belonging. Nora Drew was a deaconess there, and Richard Drew sang in the church choir. The whole family attended services every Sunday morning. They listened to the Rev. Walter Brooks urge members to serve their community.

When Charlie was two, his sister Elsie was born. Then came his brother, Joseph, in 1909, his sister Nora in 1913, and his sister Eva in 1921.

Nora and Richard Drew were attentive parents who always expected their children to do their best. Mrs. Drew had graduated from Howard University and, for several years, worked as a school teacher. She stopped working outside the home in order to give more attention to her growing children.

When urging her children to do their schoolwork or finish their chores around the house, Mrs. Drew would remind them how hard their father worked to support them.

"Don't you ever forget," Nora Drew would say, "you were cared for and educated by your father—on his knees."

Richard Drew *did* work on his knees. He was a carpet layer for the Moses Furniture Company. Mr. Drew was a friendly man with red hair, lots of freckles, and a big moustache.

Charlie's parents saw to it that the Drew children had opportunities for fun and adventure. There were books to read and lively discussions to join. There was music—both parents sang, and Mr. Drew played the piano and the guitar.

For the Drew children, there were weekend trips to the museums, historical monuments, government buildings, and theaters—all of the important sites of the nation's capital.

The Drew household was always a busy place. Mr. and Mrs. Drew taught their children to help out

with the chores at home. Nora Drew Gregory, Drew's sister, remembers that Charlie learned the basics of his surgeon's stitches early in life. One of his jobs was to mend his own clothes.

As the oldest of the Drew children, Charlie was expected not only to complete his own jobs around the house, but to help organize and direct the younger children, too. Then, at the age of 12, he got his first "real" job, and he put those organizing skills to work.

Charlie became a paper boy, selling newspapers on the busy street corners of Washington. At first, he worked alone, but soon he hired his brother, Joseph, as his assistant. Together, Charlie figured, they could sell far more papers than one boy could by himself.

But Charlie had even bigger plans. He hired six more boys, assigning a different location to each one and taking a share of their proceeds. His newspaper sales took off! Years later, Charles Drew would look back upon this early experience and claim that it had taught him much of what he knew about organizing and supervising people.

Charlie Drew went to the "separate but equal" Stevens Elementary School. He was a good student, but his real love was sports. Charlie was an outstanding athlete. When he was eight, he won the annual Fourth of July swimming meet at the neighborhood pool. Determined to do his best, Charlie practiced his swimming every afternoon. At the age of 11, he won a junior swimming championship for the entire city of Washington. And for three straight years at Stevens, he was a member of the championship baseball and basketball teams.

In 1918, when Charlie was 14, he graduated from Stevens and entered Dunbar High School. Founded in 1870, Dunbar was the first high school for African-Americans. It was named for Paul Laurence Dunbar, a black American poet and novelist.

By the time Charlie Drew enrolled, Dunbar was recognized as one of the best schools in the country. Among its modern graduates are Benjamin O. Davis, Sr., America's first black general; Robert C. Weaver, the first black Cabinet member (Secretary of Housing and Urban Development); Edward Brooke, a senator from the state of Massachusetts, and William Hastie, the first black American to become a federal district court judge.

Dunbar was known as a difficult school, requiring its students to master Greek and Latin as well as chemistry, biology, and math. Such training brought success to many Dunbar graduates when they applied to college. At a time when only 13 percent of high-school graduates continued their education, Dunbar was sending more than 75 percent of its graduates to college. Those colleges were often the best schools—Amherst, Williams, Harvard, and Yale regularly took graduates of Dunbar.

Charles Drew starred on four of Dunbar's athletic teams—football, basketball, baseball, and track. In his junior and senior years, the school awarded him the James E. Walker Medal, a prize given to the best all-around athlete and student. Drew's classmates elected him president of his senior class. He was also voted "the best athlete," "the most popular student," and "the student who did the most for the school."

When he graduated in 1922, Charles Drew was prepared for new challenges and new horizons. He accepted an athletic scholarship to Amherst College. At the age of 18, he left Washington, D.C., and headed for a small country town in western Massachusetts.

3

"Big Red"

Today, industries and businesses have changed the landscape that surrounds the village of Amherst, Massachusetts. When Charles Drew arrived there, he saw green fields and thick woods of pines and oaks. But the village of Amherst itself has changed little in the intervening years. It is still a town of narrow, tree-lined streets and small shops. The center of town is the village green. And up the hill is the campus of Amherst College.

Amherst is a small liberal arts school. Today, it enrolls both men and women. In 1922, however, Amherst was a men's school, and the student population was mostly white. Only 16 black students graduated from Amherst between 1920 and 1929.

By the time he was 18, Charlie Drew had grown into a big man—over six feet tall and weighing almost 200 pounds. He had also gained a new nickname— "Big Red." Charlie had inherited his father's reddish brown hair and light, freckled skin, and people who knew him said that when Charlie felt angry or upset, his face would flush a bright red.

Charlie began to prove himself once again as an outstanding athlete. However, after the first six weeks of classes, his grades were suffering. There is a story told about this period in his life that involves a meeting between Drew and the college dean. Concerned about the new student's grades, the dean suggested that perhaps Drew was paying too much attention to sports—and not enough attention to his studies.

Apparently, Drew thought there was a different reason for the problem. Charlie argued that he was at a disadvantage because Dunbar, a segregated school, hadn't provided him with the kinds of skills that the more privileged, white students had learned at their schools. The dean replied that Dunbar was one of the finest schools in the country and that Charles Drew had within him the tools he needed to succeed—if he was willing to work hard.

The dean went even further. He told Charlie to think about what he wanted to do with his life. If he wanted to be an athlete, then he should pursue that goal. But if Drew wanted to be something other than an athlete, he had better start studying as hard as he could. The dean ended his remarks by saying, "Mr. Drew, Negro athletes are a dime a dozen."

What the dean probably meant by his blunt statement was that Charlie Drew had the talent to be an athlete—and more than an athlete. Then, as now, very few college athletes are fortunate enough to make it to the professional leagues. And those who don't make it need to rely on other talents and interests to support themselves. Even those who do succeed usually enjoy very brief careers as athletes. The average professional athletic career lasts only about four years.

It seems that Charlie understood what the dean meant. His grades started to improve.

But he didn't give up sports. Charles Drew was the only member of his freshman class to earn a letter in a varsity sport. He excelled at track, competing in the high jump and the 120-yard high hurdles. He set an Amherst record of 15.2 seconds in the hurdles, won a national championship meet, and narrowly missed a spot on the U.S. Olympic team.

In his senior year, Drew became the captain of the Amherst track team. He was also a star halfback on the football team.

"Tuss" McLaughry, the Amherst football coach, called Drew "the best player" he ever coached. McLaughry described Drew as being "lightning fast on the getaway and dynamite on inside plays, plowing on with a second effort that brought him yardage long after he should have been stopped."

In those days, football players had to cover both offense and defense; while playing offense, running backs were allowed to throw forward passes. One of

Drew's former classmates remembers him in the 1923 game against Wesleyan, a game that the sportswriters had predicted Amherst would lose by 30 points:

> *The opening kickoff went to Drew who ran it back for a touchdown. The extra point was missed. In the second quarter, Wesleyan scored a field goal, so the score was 6-3. In the third quarter, Wesleyan scored a touchdown and kicked in the extra point. Score 10-6, Wesleyan.*
>
> *In the fourth quarter, Amherst wound up with the ball on its own 45-yard line with three seconds to go. Drew faded and faded back and finally threw a pass that knocked him off his feet. It went into the end zone—John McBride caught it for a 12-10 victory. The first play was Drew, the last play was Drew, and in between it was Wesleyan!*

In 1924, Drew's junior year, he won the Thomas Ashley Memorial Trophy for being the football team's most valuable player. And in 1925, his senior year, he was named to the All-New England and All-Eastern teams as a halfback, and the Associated Press gave Drew honorable mention status as All-American left halfback. When he graduated from Amherst in 1926, he was awarded the Howard Hill Mossman Cup as the student who had "brought the greatest honor in athletics" to the college.

But Drew wasn't always treated like a star. His wife, Lenore, recalls that, as a black athlete, Charles Drew faced obstacles on and off the playing field:

A great many people were not yet ready for black stars in a white world, and Charlie met with racial slurs both on and off the field. The insults made him flush the dangerous, dark-red color that earned him the nickname "Big Red." Charlie controlled his temper, though, for he had already decided that our people—any people—could make more real progress by "doing and showing" than by any amount of violent demonstration.

At times, the cruelty of racial prejudice hurt Drew deeply. Once, when the Amherst track team traveled to Providence, Rhode Island, for a meet with Brown University, Charlie and other black members of the squad were refused entrance to the hotel where the team planned to eat dinner. The rest of the team went ahead with their dinner plans while Charlie and the other black students ate at a cafeteria on the Brown University campus.

A similar event happened at a hotel in Boston, Massachusetts, where the Amherst football team had made reservations to spend the night. The desk clerk refused to give rooms to the black members of the team. This time, Drew's coach objected. "Boston's got more than one hotel," Tuss McLaughry boomed to the clerk. With that announcement, he led the entire team out of the hotel.

Prejudice could be found on the Amherst College campus, too, as an incident during Drew's junior year illustrates. Each year, 12 Amherst students shared the honor of being selected to join the Scarab Society, a club for seniors recognized for all-around excellence. Each outgoing Scarab, before he graduated, selected the person who would take his place. Most students agreed that Drew deserved to be a Scarab. But he wasn't chosen. As a former classmate recalls, "All of us knew he would have been if he had been white. There was stunned disbelief in the college."

In his own summary of his college days, written 20 years later in a letter to Charles Cole, then president of Amherst College, Charles Drew stated that his "major interest at this stage" was still athletics. But during his senior year, he began to think about his academic future beyond Amherst. He began to think about becoming a doctor.

Two events may have inspired Drew to consider a medical career. First, his younger sister Elsie had died of tuberculosis while Charles was still in high school. That tragedy seems to have ignited in him a desire to help others by becoming a doctor. Then, at Amherst, Drew received a thigh injury in a football game. When the wound became seriously infected, he went to a nearby hospital for treatment. There, Drew became interested in his own treatment and, while he accompanied the doctor on hospital rounds, that of other patients as well.

By the time he graduated from Amherst in 1926, Drew had decided to apply to medical school. Money was his biggest problem. His scholarship to Amherst had paid for most of his expenses there, and student loans had covered the rest. Having graduated, he now had to work to pay off the loans, saving whatever he could toward the cost of medical school. So Charles Drew went back to the Washington area to find a job.

He became a teacher of biology and chemistry at Morgan College, a school in Baltimore, Maryland. He was also asked to serve as Director of Athletics. To earn some extra money, Drew refereed at basketball and football games.

Drew remained at Morgan College for two years. He is credited with transforming groups of "average" athletes into outstanding sports teams. As Drew himself once proudly stated, "Teams begun at the time compiled one of the most brilliant records of any college in America. In one period, 54 consecutive football games were played without a single loss."

"Drew was that kind of coach," historian Charles Wynes noted. "Later, he would become that kind of teacher and trainer of surgeons. He was able to inspire the merely competent to become good, the good to become better, and the better to become the best."

By 1928, Drew had saved enough money. He was ready to apply to medical school.

At that time, the best American medical schools rarely accepted black students. Blacks who aspired to become doctors had, for the most part, two schools to choose from, and both of them, although not officially segregated schools, were attended predominantly by blacks. These were Meharry Medical College, located in Nashville, Tennessee, and the Howard University Medical School, in Washington, D.C.

Drew's first choice was Howard University. As a student there, he would be able to live at home with his family, thus reducing expenses. He also applied to Harvard University, then considered by many to have the country's best medical school. Harvard accepted Drew, but informed him that the class for the current year was full. If he wanted to attend Harvard Medical School, Drew would have to wait another year before enrolling. But he had postponed medical school for two years already, and Drew did not want to put it off any longer.

Unfortunately, Howard, his first choice, decided against him. They rejected his application, saying that Drew had not earned the required number of English credits at Amherst. However, they did offer him a job as assistant football coach. According to his brother, Joe, Drew was so angry that he stormed, "Someday I'll come back to Howard and run the damned place!"

Eventually, that's exactly what he did. But first he applied to the medical school at McGill University in Montreal, Canada. Unlike Harvard, McGill had room for him immediately; unlike Howard, the Canadian school found his credentials satisfactory. So it was in Canada that "Big Red" became Dr. Charles Drew.

4

Dr. Charles Drew

Athletic excellence provided Drew with an image of himself that served as a guide throughout his life. He was a sprinter—a runner who needs to muster up great bursts of energy to run short races at top speed. In later years, when people would ask him how he managed to accomplish so much, Drew would simply shrug and say, "I'm a sprinter!"

Drew's years at McGill called for his "sprinting" spirit. He was a determined, driven student. After two years of hard work and high-ranking marks, he was elected, during his third year, to Alpha Omega Alpha, an honor society for outstanding medical students. In 1933, Drew's final year at McGill, he was second in his class of 137 students and was awarded the Williams Prize, given to the student who scores the highest on an annual examination.

Drew's academic success did not mean that he had lost his interest in athletics. He competed in four

events for the McGill track team—the broad jump, the high jump, and the low and high hurdles—and won Canadian championships in all four events. He was elected captain of the McGill track team in 1931. This honor, coupled with his captainship of the track team at Amherst, made him the first black American to lead varsity teams at two major colleges.

Money was again a burden for him, and Drew often worried about having to withdraw from school. His parents sent him whatever they could afford, and he took a job as a waiter. His old friend and football coach, Tuss McLaughry, loaned him some money and urged Drew's old classmates to do the same.

On December 31, 1929, Charles Drew sat alone in his room while his friends were out celebrating New Year's Eve. In a "letter" addressed to the "Spirit of the New Year, 1930," he wrote of his troubles:

> *Today I haven't been hungry. I was well dressed. I am not sick and have no great sorrow, yet I have felt poverty today as I have never felt it before. I have a dollar. Tonight I wanted to join the merry-making in some form or another so bad that my very heart ached. I couldn't go very far on a dollar, not even alone.*

His pride had led him to refuse when one of his classmates offered him a loan so that he might join the fun. As he continued his "letter" to the New Year, he spoke of that pride:

> *I never ask favors. That is one of the things I am proud of. Rightly or wrongly proud, I don't know. This I know—that this pride sustains me when otherwise I would sink. . . . My classmates today could not understand why I wouldn't go to the dance with them tonight. When I told them frankly that I was broke, they simply thought I had overspent my allowance or my check hadn't come in, or something to that effect. They didn't understand that while $10 to some of them will mean—well, just $10 and maybe a note to Dad, that to me it means a whole week's living, or from my father it would mean an actual sacrifice for the rest of my family.*

Stubbornly insisting on his independence, Drew did not want to be "obligated to anyone in any way." "I am the equal of any man I meet," he wrote.

But pride has its price, he knew, in loneliness and despair. "Here I am," Drew said, "a stranger amongst strangers in a strange land, broke, busted, almost disgusted, doing my family no good, myself little that is now demonstrable."

Still, Drew was determined to persevere. "I must go on," he wrote. "I must finish what I have started."

One of the things Drew had started was the study of blood. His interest in blood research was due to the influence of one of his teachers, a visiting professor from England named Dr. John Beattie. Beattie taught bacteriology, the study of diseases caused by bacteria, and worked on blood research at the laboratories of Montreal General Hospital. Beattie was investigating the role of blood transfusions—the process by which blood from one person is given to another person—in the treatment of patients with bacterial infections.

The study of blood transfusions was, at the time of Beattie's research efforts, a new and exciting topic. In 1930, during Drew's third year of medical school, an American doctor named Karl Landsteiner won the Nobel Prize in Medicine for his discovery of the four different types of human blood: Type A, Type B, Type AB, and Type O. (Landsteiner had actually made his historic discovery 30 years earlier. He was continuing his research, hoping to make blood transfusions safe and effective.)

Whatever the type, human blood is made up of four components: red blood cells, white blood cells, platelets, and plasma. Landsteiner found that the four types of blood differ because the red blood cells contain different kinds of, or different combinations of, chemicals called antigens. If a person with one type of blood receives a transfusion containing another type of blood, he or she may have a dangerous reaction.

Landsteiner's discovery meant that doctors could at last determine the specific type of blood that a patient needed. At Montreal General, Beattie was responsible for testing the blood of potential donors to make sure that the blood type was compatible with that of potential recipients.

Although doctors could now test blood for compatibility, they faced another problem: how to bank blood so that it would be in ready supply whenever it was needed.

Blood that is drawn from a donor and then given to a recipient is called whole blood. Whole blood is extremely perishable. It must be kept refrigerated, and even then, it lasts for only several weeks. After that, the red blood cells begin to break down; the blood is no longer useable.

In 1930, when Beattie and Drew began to work on the problem of blood storage, whole blood could be preserved for only seven days. As a result, surgical procedures might have to be postponed until a donor could be found. Worse, patients who lost a great deal of blood as a result of an accident might die before a compatible donor was found.

In the 1930s, researchers continued to study the problem of how to bank blood more effectively. And Charles Drew used the knowledge he had begun to gather, through his work with John Beattie, to help solve that problem.

In 1933, Drew graduated from McGill University Medical School with honors, receiving both a Doctor of Medicine and a Master of Surgery degree. Dr. Drew spent the next year completing his internship at the Royal Victoria Hospital and Montreal General, where he continued his work in blood research with Beattie. Drew finished his residency in internal medicine at Montreal General Hospital in 1935. Now he had all the requirements that he needed to practice medicine.

But having chosen to specialize in surgery, Drew had to participate in an additional residency program. He could have been awarded a surgical residency at any of the major medical schools. But Charles Drew had decided that there was only one place he wanted to go—home to Washington, D.C.

His father had died earlier that year, and Drew wanted to go home to take care of his family. He also planned to help other black men and women become doctors. He felt a debt to those who had struggled to create new opportunities for his generation; now he wanted to repay that debt by doing the same for those who came after him. So Charles Drew applied again to the school that had once rejected him, the Howard University Medical School.

Howard University was established in 1867. The school was named after General Oliver Otis Howard, the first director of the Freedmen's Bureau, the federal agency established after the Civil War to help former slaves ("freed men"). Howard's aim was to educate freed blacks. From the start, however, the university was almost always badly in need of funds. The same condition was true of Freedmen's Hospital, the teaching and clinical facility associated with the Howard University Medical School.

Freedmen's Hospital began as a makeshift clinic organized by the federal government in 1862 to give medical assistance to the thousands of former slaves who flooded into Washington, D.C., during the Civil War. In 1869, a new, enlarged facility was established on the campus of Howard University.

Set up as a "charity" hospital, Freedmen's was not authorized to treat private, paying patients until 1912. Strapped for funds, the hospital was clearly a "separate and unequal" medical facility. Even its own president, Mordecai Johnson, referred to it as a "Jim Crow shack." But for many years, Freedmen's was the only hospital in Washington, D.C., where black doctors could treat private patients.

Howard University accepted Charles Drew as an instructor in pathology, the study of disease. In 1936, he worked as a faculty assistant in surgery while completing his residency at Freedmen's Hospital. In 1937, he was promoted to instructor of surgery at Howard and made an assistant surgeon at Freedmen's.

The Howard University Medical School was supported by both government grants and private funds.

Private groups provided funds, or fellowships, for the most promising teachers at Howard to pursue further training at major American medical schools and their associated hospitals. One of the Howard teachers to receive such a fellowship was Charles Drew.

In the fall of 1938, only three years after returning home, Charles Drew headed to New York City. There, he would continue his research at Columbia University and complete an advanced residency program in surgery at an affiliated teaching facility, the Columbia-Presbyterian Medical Center.

5

Blood Pioneer

Arriving at Columbia in 1938, Drew reported to Dr. Allen O. Whipple, the head of the Department of Surgery. Whipple assigned the young doctor to work with Dr. John Scudder. Scudder, an assistant professor of surgery, headed a group of doctors involved in blood research.

Drew's knowledge of blood transfusions, gained through his research at McGill, made him a perfect selection for this team. Scudder asked his assistant to work on the crucial problem related to blood transfusions: how to preserve and bank blood for future use. Scudder's goal was to establish a blood bank at the Columbia-Presbyterian Medical Center.

Drew carefully studied the research of previous blood pioneers, including Karl Landsteiner, who had won the Nobel Prize for discovering the four types of human blood; T. L. W. Bischoff, a German scientist who first performed transfusions with stored blood;

and a Belgian doctor, A. Hustin, who tried to preserve whole blood by adding the chemical sodium citrate to it. (Sodium citrate, it was later learned, hinders the blood's ability to clot. A person who receives a transfusion of blood with sodium citrate in it might bleed to death.)

Drew also reviewed the efforts of other scientists who had tried to create blood banks. An American doctor, Bernard Fantus, had invented the term "blood bank" and, in 1937, had established the first American facility for the storage of whole blood at Cook County Hospital in Chicago, Illinois. However, doctors from the Soviet Union had experimented with methods of blood preservation years earlier.

One Soviet scientist, Dr. S. S. Yudin, succeeded in drawing blood from cadavers (dead bodies), storing it, and then using it for transfusions. By 1938, the time that Drew began to research methods of blood storage and preservation, Yudin had already performed more than 2,000 successful transfusions with cadaver blood. (Cadaver blood can be preserved for a period of only 10 days, however.)

Drew pored over these reports. In an article published in the *American Review of Soviet Medicine*, Drew gave credit to the Soviet scientists "for supplying the early work and most of the fundamental knowledge which has to a large degree been responsible for the widespread creation of the blood and plasma banks."

In the same report, he also cited two other scientists, Duran Jorda and Norman Bethune, who organized a blood banking program to serve the critical need for blood transfusions that arose during the Spanish Civil War (1936-1939).

Drew was compiling and building on the work of these scientists. He tested and retested blood samples, trying to determine how and why whole blood breaks down. He reduced whole blood to its four elements—red blood cells, white blood cells, platelets, and plasma—to study how each component might play a part in lengthening the "life" of whole blood.

More than half of every drop of whole blood is made up of a yellowish, watery liquid called plasma. It carries nutrients to the cells of the body. It helps remove waste products from cells, too, carrying the wastes to the kidneys, where they are filtered out of the plasma and excreted by the body. Fibrinogen, a chemical that helps blood to clot, and globulin, which helps the body to fight infection, are found in plasma.

Plasma is only one component of blood, and, by itself, it cannot supply all the benefits of whole blood. But in an emergency, a transfusion of plasma can save a person's life.

As a source for transfusions, plasma has another advantage that whole blood lacks. The substances that determine blood types are found only in red blood

cells, not plasma. Any person—no matter what blood type—can receive plasma from anyone else.

Equally important, plasma is not as perishable as whole blood. It can be stored for a much longer time than whole blood can. Plasma can also be dehydrated. (Dehydration is the process that removes water from the plasma and leaves a residue of plasma powder.) This process allows plasma to be easily transported and stored. The plasma powder is returned to liquid form by adding water before it is transfused into a person's body.

The use of plasma is particularly helpful when blood transfusions are needed by many people at the same time. On a battlefield, for instance, it can save the life of a wounded soldier by combating shock. It can be administered quickly, even if a person's blood type is not known. Since it can be processed into a powdered form, plasma can be collected and stored in advance of a disaster. For these reasons, the use of plasma seemed to be the key to blood banking.

Drew continued to study plasma as a substitute for whole blood. He worked 18-hour days, performing surgery in the mornings and spending the afternoons at his research. It must have seemed a welcome relief, then, when his old friend, Dr. Numa Adams, then dean of the Howard University Medical School, invited him to speak on the subject of blood transfusions at a medical clinic held annually at a hospital in Tuskegee, Alabama.

For Drew, the meeting was a chance to visit with his friends and colleagues from Howard University. He joined the Howard doctors in Washington, D.C., and together they began the long drive to Alabama. On the way, they spent the night in Atlanta, Georgia, with W. Mercer Cook, one of Drew's old friends from Amherst College.

Cook had arranged a party for his guests. There, at the dinner table, Charles Drew met Lenore Robbins, a home economics teacher at Spelman College. "He came into my life at a party in Atlanta on an April evening in 1939," Lenore recalled.

From the first, Lenore realized that Charles Drew was no ordinary man:

> *The moment I saw him I knew he was a man to be reckoned with. He seemed to be from another—a more old-fashioned and courtly—time and place. He listened with fatherly interest to the hopes and problems that some of us teachers poured out to him. "Just keep dreaming high," he told us. "We'll make the kind of world we want."*

And Lenore certainly made a positive impression on Drew, for the young doctor had already made up his mind. He wanted to marry her.

Drew went on to Tuskegee the next morning as planned and delivered his lecture on transfusions to the doctors assembled at the conference. But then he parted company with Dean Adams and the other doctors from Howard University. Charles Drew boarded the first train headed to Atlanta.

By the time he arrived at the campus of Spelman College, it was one o'clock in the morning. The lights were out, and everyone was asleep. Banging on the front door of Lenore's dormitory, Drew awakened the housemother and insisted on seeing Lenore. After he explained that he couldn't come back the next morning—his train for New York was scheduled to leave in an hour—the startled housemother reluctantly agreed to get Lenore.

Many years later, Lenore Robbins Drew remembered that hour well. "I went down to meet Dr. Drew on the moonlit campus," she recalled. "He proposed to me then and there. Six months later, we married and began our life together in New York City."

During the months between their engagement in April and their marriage in September, Drew wrote many letters to Lenore. These letters offer a glimpse into his deepest thoughts and emotions.

In one of his earliest letters to her, he described the feelings he experienced while listening to Marian Anderson, the great black opera singer, perform at a concert in Washington, D.C. Anderson was originally scheduled to sing at Constitution Hall, but the invitation had been withdrawn at the last minute because she was black. The concert was moved to the steps of the Lincoln Memorial. Of her performance that day, Drew wrote:

> *In all my life I have never seen such an impressive thing. With the soft rays of pink sun gleaming against the white marble beauty of that magnificent structure and reflecting itself in the long still pool of water that stretches off toward the Washington Monument, she raised her exquisite voice in song and lifted with a sweep of melody a whole race to higher levels of thought, feeling, and hope.*

In a letter written soon afterward, Drew spoke of his own hopes and dreams. He said that he wanted to be "a good doctor and able surgeon." Then he told Lenore of the aspiration that meant the most to him. "In my wildest moments," Drew wrote, he imagined that he might play "some part in establishing a real school of thought among Negro physicians and guiding younger fellows to levels of accomplishment not yet attained by any of us."

On August 9, 1939, Charles Drew watched as the doors of the Columbia-Presbyterian blood bank were opened. He was 35 years old. John Scudder called him not only "my most brilliant student, but one of the greatest clinical scientists of the first half of the twentieth century."

The next month, on September 23, Charles Drew and Lenore Robbins were married. But Drew's busy schedule would not permit a honeymoon. There was a thesis to write, surgery to perform, and a blood bank to run.

A year later, Charles Drew submitted the results of his research. Scudder thought that Drew's thesis, titled "Banked Blood: A Study in Blood Preservation," was "a masterpiece." He praised Drew's work as "one of the most distinguished essays ever written, both in form and content."

In June of 1940, Drew was awarded the Doctor of Science in Medicine degree. He was the first African-American doctor to receive this distinction. Later that year, he passed the written part of his examination for certification by the American Board of Surgery.

Lenore used to chide her husband for trying to manage so many important projects. "You can't do all these things at once," she protested. "You've got to slow down!"

Drew would just grin and say, "I'm a sprinter, Lenore, remember?"

6

Time of War

1940 was a time of new beginnings for the Drews. Charles returned to Howard, where he was made an assistant professor in surgery. He was also appointed a surgeon at Freedmen's Hospital. Proud of his recent accomplishments, especially the Doctor of Science in Medicine degree, Charles Drew was glad to be home.

"It feels like the day after a big race is won," he wrote shortly before he received the degree. "When it is all over, it is just another medal in the box—and we look forward to next season's competition. My next big 'meet' is at Howard."

That fall witnessed another beginning for Charles and Lenore Drew, with the birth of their first child, "Bebe" Roberta Drew. ("Bebe" came from B.B., standing for "blood bank.")

But Charles Drew had to postpone his "meet" at Howard. He was home for only three months.

Drew returned to New York at the summons of John Scudder, who was now working with a group called the Blood Transfusion Betterment Association. The association sought to provide blood transfusions for the victims of World War II. As the war casualties mounted, the need for blood became critical.

On June 12, 1940, an emergency meeting of the Blood Transfusion Betterment Association had been held at the New York Academy of Medicine. Drew and Scudder both attended. The reports from the war front made it clear that there was no time to waste. The members of the association decided to launch a "Blood for Britain" program.

When Scudder declined the position of medical supervisor of the blood program, the job was offered to Drew. He accepted and was granted a four-month leave of absence from Howard University. Drew left home in September to begin work on the "Blood for Britain" campaign.

By the time Drew arrived in New York, the Blood Transfusion Betterment Association had secured the financial support of the American Red Cross to establish the "Blood for Britain" program. In August, the program had officially begun when a small shipment of liquid plasma was sent to Britain. The association also started a research program to use dried plasma as a whole blood substitute.

America was not yet fighting in the war, but two of its allies, the British and the French, were suffering heavy losses as they tried to repel the German forces. France was near defeat, and Britain was under constant attack by a prolonged German air assault called "the blitz" (the shortened form of the German word, "blitzkrieg," which means "lightning war").

Every night for four weeks, the German airplanes swarmed in the skies above London, bombing the city to ruins. The British urgently needed to find a source of preserved blood to treat the injured. They turned to America for help.

On September 3, Dr. John Beattie, Drew's former teacher at McGill, sent him an urgent telegram. Beattie was now the chief of blood transfusion services for Britain's Royal Air Force. He knew that his country's supply of blood was nearly depleted. Hoping that his former colleague in blood research might be able to help, Beattie cabled Drew a desperate message:

> *Could you secure five thousand ampoules dried plasma for transfusion work immediately and follow this by equal quantity in three to four weeks? Contents each ampoule should represent about one pint whole plasma.*

It was an impossible request. There wasn't that much dried plasma in the whole world.

Better than anyone else, Charles Drew knew the problems involved in collecting plasma. The need for safe processing procedures was crucial. Scudder and Drew had been working with liquid plasma, conducting numerous clinical tests at Columbia-Presbyterian. As before, Drew studied the research of many other scientists, including John R. Elliott's work with liquid plasma and Edwin J. Cohn's studies on dried plasma.

The first problem Drew faced was how to collect as much blood as possible in the shortest amount of time. Eight hospitals in New York City were processing blood donors every day for the "Blood for Britain" campaign, but even they could not handle the number of donors needed.

To solve this problem, Drew came up with the idea of using mobile collection units. Trucks equipped with portable refrigerators were sent to every quarter of the city to collect blood. (Today, the Red Cross still uses such vehicles during its blood drives.)

Another of Drew's major concerns was that each pint of whole blood be processed into plasma under a strictly monitored procedure. Safe guidelines would protect the blood supply against contamination. Drew established the processing guidelines himself, setting up a laboratory at Columbia-Presbyterian where the work would be done under his supervision.

Drew reviewed recent studies on blood processing techniques—and then he went beyond them. He

experimented with even more current, and sometimes untested, procedures. For example, he learned that the British had been able to obtain plasma from blood by using an adaption of a cream separator, the machine that farmers use to separate cream from milk. Drew ordered two of the machines from Great Britain. Once Drew tested them and found them to be useful, he had several more machines made in the United States so massive quantities of plasma could be processed each day.

Drew's expertise in blood banking, however, was only partly responsible for his success. He was a tireless worker and, according to the Blood Transfusion Association, "an excellent organizer" of people. "Our problems have vanished," the association commented, "since Drew has been in charge." By the beginning of October 1940, one month after Charles Drew assumed the role of medical supervisor for America's "Blood for Britain" program, Britain was receiving regular air shipments of large quantities of plasma.

More than 14,000 donations of plasma followed over the next four months. But in late October 1940, the British government announced that, following the guidelines of the American program, it had successfully established its own blood collection and processing centers. As of January 1941, the British would be able to take over the job of supplying their casualties with blood transfusions.

Charles Drew succeeded through hard work and unwavering commitment, and the personal costs were high. To cut expenses, he had lived in a room at a YMCA in New York City, while his wife and their daughter stayed at home near Howard University.

In a letter he wrote to Lenore in December 1940, Drew expressed concern about the war and sadness over the family separation. "One cannot tell what the future of anything is going to be in times as turbulent as these," Drew observed.

But he told Lenore that the "Blood for Britain" program was coming to an end. He should be "home for good" soon.

As much as he looked forward to being home for good, the turbulent times demanded something more from Charles Drew. It was becoming obvious that the United States could not stay out of the war forever. To be ready for the conflict, the country needed to build up its own supply of banked blood and plasma. Drew saw the crisis coming, too. When his four-month leave of absence from Howard had nearly expired, Drew asked for and was granted an extension.

When the U.S. government asked the American Red Cross to undertake a nationwide project similar to "Blood for Britain," the Red Cross named Charles Drew assistant director of a three-month program to "experiment in mass production." Unlike the "Blood for Britain" program, which processed thousands of pints of liquid plasma, the American program would produce dried plasma.

The liquid plasma sent to England had been used primarily to meet the medical crisis of the wounded in the city of London. But the program for the American military troops had to be planned for battlefield conditions. Since dried plasma could be stored for longer periods of time and did not require refrigeration, it was a more practical solution.

Although research in dried plasma had increased in recent years, there was no tested process for mass production. It was Drew's job to develop that process in time to meet the country's demand for a safe and reliable supply of plasma.

The "Blood for Britain" program was designed to supply an immediate and critical need for blood. By contrast, America was not yet a nation at war. The new American program was still, at the time of its birth, an "insurance policy."

But it was largely through Drew's efforts that an adequate blood supply was ready when the United States entered the war in 1941. The trial program that Drew worked on was the basis of successful collection efforts at the national level.

In providing blood for the U.S. military, however, Drew faced a problem that was far more troublesome than mass-producing supplies of dried plasma. The U.S. War Department (now the Defense Department)

insisted that the blood supply for the armed forces be collected from white donors only. Only "white" blood would be accepted by the U.S. armed forces. Such a policy clearly reflected the Jim Crow regulations that existed throughout the armed forces at the time.

Drew reacted to this blood-collection policy with disbelief and frustration. "Charlie couldn't sit still for this affront," Lenore Drew recalled. "It was an affront both to his race and to science."

Charles Drew was reported to have denounced this policy as unscientific. "No difficulties have been shown to exist between the bloods of different races," he said, "which would in any way counter-indicate the use of blood from an individual of one race to an individual of another race."

In other words, Drew argued that blood doesn't differ among races. The only differences that occur in blood are at the chemical level—the differences that make the blood groupings Type A, B, AB, or O. A black person's Type A blood is the same as a white person's Type A blood.

Many people protested against the "white blood" policy, but there was little government response. In January 1942, the U.S. armed forces announced that blood from black donors would be collected, but that the plasma produced from "black" blood would be segregated: it would be used only in transfusions for black soldiers. With this new policy, the military gave a new meaning to the concept of "separate but equal."

Tired and frustrated, Charles Drew happily saw his leave of absence from Howard University expire in April 1941. With the national blood plasma project under way, Drew was ready to leave his post with the American Red Cross and return to Howard University. He was ready to go home for good.

7

A Tough Teacher

In April 1941, Drew went to The Johns Hopkins University in Baltimore, Maryland, for the oral part of the American Board of Surgery examination. He was asked to discuss fluid balance in the human body.

This was a subject that Drew knew well. Essential to the study of blood transfusions, it had been one of the major topics of his research with John Scudder at Columbia University. His responses to the questions were extremely complex, reflecting a knowledge that went far beyond that of the surgeon questioning him.

In fact, the questioner had to call upon other surgeons to help him assess Drew's answers. Needless to say, Charles Drew passed his examination, becoming one of the first black doctors to receive certification by the American Board of Surgery. Several months later, in October, the certification board made Drew himself an examiner—the first black surgeon to be appointed to this position.

That fall, Drew was made professor of surgery at Howard University and chief surgeon at Freedmen's Hospital. It was the beginning of what he considered to be his most important work—the training of young black surgeons.

He was a tough teacher, demanding that his students work just as hard as he did. One of his former students, Dr. Merle Hereford, said, "When Dr. Drew got with people, he made them believe things could be done that they just didn't believe otherwise."

Sometimes, Drew's friendliness was the source of inspiration. "Drew possessed a sense of geniality that was magnetic," historian Charles Wynes reports. "The effect—as those who were there still remember—was magical." Other times, it was his sense of discipline and drive that motivated his students.

Drew instilled in his students not only a determination to do their best work, but a sense of pride. A colleague of his at Freedmen's, Dr. Samuel L. Bullock, remembers that Drew was a rather "severe" teacher. "He was a perfectionist," Bullock added. "He thrived on doing things—and having others do them—that he could take pride in."

Drew was critical of students who dressed sloppily, he was stern with those who chatted or joked while on duty, and when he discovered that some of his young doctors were gambling during their breaks, he forbade such activities on the hospital premises.

And Drew took pride in his students. Once, while making his rounds in the hospital, he stopped to examine a woman who was under the care of one of his junior medical students. Drew told the woman that she would have to have an operation very shortly. She replied that she would not agree to the surgery until she had talked to her doctor. Drew was surprised that this woman had more confidence in a medical student than in the chief surgeon. But he was impressed that his student had done such a good job of gaining the patient's trust.

The goal behind his teaching was two-fold: first, to train doctors capable of meeting the highest standards; and second, to place those doctors in positions of professional leadership. Drew said that he wanted to place his students "in strategic positions throughout the nation so that they could, in turn, act as seeds for the growth of other centers."

Drew stayed in contact with the surgeons he sent across the country. To one of his students, Dr. Jack White, he wrote:

> *I know you must feel that I have sent you off to the far northland and left you to work out your destiny as best you could without further interest on our part. This is not true. We still love you and are extremely interested in what you do, what you think, and what you plan for the future.*

As a teacher, Drew pursued his goals with a firm hand, but his students remember him as warm, just, and understanding. From Charles Drew, they learned more than surgical techniques. They received a lesson in the meaning of courage and commitment as well.

But overseeing the training programs for young surgeons was a demanding job, one that took up most of Drew's energy. He often had to sacrifice time with his own growing family. A second daughter, Charlene Rosella, was born in July of 1941. In February of 1944, she was followed by a third daughter, Rhea Sylvia. In October of 1945, a fourth child, Charles Richard Drew, Jr., was born.

Although the four children didn't spend a great deal of time with their father, Drew was, according to Lenore, "a hearty man who loved to romp with his children, to sing, and play the piano, saxophone, and even the ukulele." He referred to his family as "this little band of Drews."

Lenore Drew understood her husband, and she supported his commitment to the medical profession. "I gave up expecting that Charlie would ever settle down to normal," Lenore wrote in 1978. "Although he loved his home life with me and our four children, it was a luxury he seldom had time to enjoy."

"For this sprinter," Lenore observed, "there was always another race to run, another hurdle to clear."

Drew was aware that his wife made sacrifices of her own. In a letter from New York, dated February 4, 1941, he shared that understanding with her:

For you, I know, it has been a disappointing period. Our separation has caused us to miss much that we might have shared together. For this I am sorry.

Many of the days and nights have been lonely here for me. I know that they have been much more lonely for you, but from time immemorial men who have beat out new paths into unknown regions have had to strike out alone, leaving all that was dear behind.

These have been new paths that I have been treading, Lenore, as new as the uncharted seas that the early sailors defied, as strange as the new lands early explorers mapped while good wives waited in fear and loneliness lest the wandering one fail to return.

Although Drew was now busy with teaching, his fame as a pioneer in medical research continued to follow him. In 1942, while again attending the annual medical clinic in Tuskegee, he received the E. S. Jones Award for Research in Medical Science. In 1943, Virginia State College presented him with an honorary Doctor of Science degree. And, in 1945, the National Association for the Advancement of Colored People

(NAACP) presented him with the Spingarn Medal, an award given for "the highest or noblest achievement by an American Negro." (Drew was the first doctor to be given this award. Other medal recipients have included George Washington Carver and Martin Luther King, Jr.)

In 1947, Drew was awarded an honorary Doctor of Science degree by Amherst College. The president of the college, Charles Cole, wrote Drew to request some biographical information on which to base his remarks at the award ceremony.

Drew sent back a brief, modest outline of his life. The final paragraph is perhaps the clearest statement of Charles Drew's own estimate of his contribution to health and medicine:

Since being here at Howard University, most of our attention has been devoted to organizing the training system at first for surgeons, and later for all branches of medicine. At present, as Professor and Head of the Department of Surgery at Howard University, and as Chief Surgeon and Medical Director of Freedmen's Hospital, there is very little time for research, but the boys whom we are now helping to train, I believe, in time will constitute my greatest contribution to medicine.

It seemed that by the late 1940s, Charles Drew, still a young man, had fulfilled all of his professional ambitions. But there was one goal he was not able to achieve. Despite Drew's prominence as a surgeon and professor, and his historic research accomplishments, he was never granted membership in the American Medical Association (AMA).

The American Medical Association is a national organization of doctors. Founded in 1847 "to promote the science and art of medicine and the betterment of the public health," it attempts to establish standards to govern a doctor's medical education and practice, insuring the quality of medical care. Membership in the AMA is a sign of a doctor's professional standing.

To gain membership in the AMA, a doctor must be accepted by one of 54 local chapters. But Drew, despite his outstanding credentials, was not admitted. The chapter that served the Washington, D.C., area refused to accept black doctors.

Drew protested the unfairness of this decision in letter after letter to the AMA. He called this policy of racial discrimination "a dark page" in the history of the AMA. In January 1947, he wrote:

> At Howard University, for many years no physician has been considered for professorial or associate professor rank in the preclinical area who has not earned a Ph.D. in his special field. In Freedmen's Hospital, the teaching hospital for the clinical years, a man must have successfully

passed his specialty board to be considered for the position of assistant professor. The chief of every department and subdivision in the department is a certified specialist in name and practice.

Match these standards with those of the great hospitals of the land and they will be found good, but the AMA will not grant [black doctors] the privilege of discussing common problems with fellow physicians in the learned councils of the American Medical Association, now celebrating its one hundredth birthday.

One hundred years of racial bigotry, . . . one hundred years of gross disinterest in a large section of the American people whose medical voice it purports to be.

It was "a sorry record," Drew said, "one hundred years with no progress to report."

Personally hurt by this rejection, Drew found it even more alarming in a general sense. Doctors who were not members of the AMA would always have to face questions about their medical qualifications. At certain hospitals only AMA members were allowed to practice. If Drew's black students could never acquire the professional respect they deserved because they were denied membership in the AMA, then the walls of bigotry that Charles Drew had been attempting to break down would stay in place. "Negro physicians are a real and vital part of American medicine," Drew insisted. He argued that "they should no longer have to explain on every application blank why they are not eligible for membership in the AMA."

Such a racist policy, Drew claimed, was an insult to African-American doctors:

> *It is an unwarranted stigma. It is a cause of repeated humiliation. It is a constant indictment of the principles on which the American Medical Association is supposedly founded.*

The AMA stood behind its policy. The association would not interfere with the membership policies of local chapters. Finally, in 1952, the Washington, D.C., chapter of the American Medical Association agreed to accept black members. In 1968, the AMA voted to forbid racial discrimination at any level.

It was a welcome change, but it did not come in time for Charles Drew.

8

A Handful of Years

The only trip that could be considered even close to a vacation for Charles Drew occurred in the summer of 1949, when he traveled to Europe. He was one of four doctors appointed by the Surgeon General of the U.S. Army to evaluate the standards of the medical facilities on military bases there. He fulfilled his responsibilities and also took some time to enjoy the sights of Germany, Austria, France, and England.

Drew wrote many lengthy letters home, sharing the sights of Europe with Lenore. It was clear that he missed an ordinary life. From Paris, he wrote his wife, "Someday we must see this place together."

But once back at home, Drew resumed the hectic pattern of his life. As in the past, he decided to attend the annual medical clinic held in Tuskegee, Alabama. The clinic was scheduled to begin on Monday, April 3, 1950.

Drew and three other doctors from Freedmen's—Drs. Samuel L. Bullock, John R. Ford, and Walter R. Johnson—planned to drive to Alabama, leaving from Washington on March 31. They had scheduled a late departure because Drew was the keynote speaker at the Howard University student council banquet that evening. The doctors decided to leave after midnight and take turns driving throughout the night.

Drew arrived home close to midnight and took a brief nap. Then, he said good-bye to Lenore and met his traveling companions. The long trip didn't begin until almost two o'clock on the morning of April 1, 1950. Dr. Bullock took the first shift. Drew began driving around sunrise, as the four doctors approached the border between Virginia and North Carolina.

Exhausted, Drew fell asleep at the wheel. Near Burlington, North Carolina, the car swerved off the road. Drew evidently awakened and tried to steer the car back onto the road, but the vehicle crashed, turning over three times.

Dr. Johnson, who was not hurt, freed Dr. Bullock, who was wedged inside the car but had suffered only a cut hand in the accident. Dr. Ford, thrown from the car when it crashed, suffered a broken arm and some serious cuts. But Charles Drew had caught his foot under the brake pedal when the car began to roll over, and his leg was nearly severed. He was barely alive.

Drew's friends called an ambulance, which took him to the Alamance General Hospital in Burlington. The doctors there worked to save his life, giving him, among other forms of treatment, a blood transfusion. But it was too late. Charles Drew died at the age of 45.

The medical world and the many people whose lives he had touched were, of course, devastated by the news. Messages of condolence came to Lenore Drew from all over the world. Many were eloquent statements regarding her husband's accomplishments.

In many others, the writers expressed the pride they felt for having been his friend, colleague, teacher, or student. One former student, Dr. Asa G. Yancey, wrote, "Doctor Drew was the greatest teacher I have ever known. His sense of justice and purity of heart were without error. I wish to share your feelings."

Thousands of people came to Drew's funeral. It was held at the Nineteenth Street Baptist Church, the church he had attended as a child. Mordecai Johnson, the president of Howard University, spoke for everyone who knew Charles Richard Drew. "Here we have what rarely happens in history," Johnson said, "a life which crowds into a handful of years significance so great, men will never forget it."

Some of Drew's colleagues, friends, and former classmates established a memorial fund to provide for his widow and four children, to continue research in blood chemistry, and to support the medical training of African-American doctors.

Amherst College created a scholarship fund in his name. Appropriately, the first student to receive one of the Charles Drew scholarships to Amherst wanted to become a doctor. Like Drew, he was also a student who earned a varsity letter on the football field.

Charles Drew left behind a legacy of achievement and inspiration. Today, due to his historic research, every major hospital has a blood bank. Transfusions of blood plasma are widely used to prevent shock in surgical patients. They are the leading treatment for patients recovering from serious burns.

During World War II, the American Red Cross collected millions of pints of blood. These donations saved the lives of thousands of wounded servicemen. And the Red Cross continues to use the methods that Drew established to collect and process blood, including the familiar bloodmobiles, modern versions of the original mobile blood-collection units.

Inspired by Drew's teaching and example, many of his students went on to prominent medical positions. Some became teachers as well, training a new generation of doctors. Hospitals and medical schools have been named for Drew, including the Charles R. Drew Postgraduate Medical School in Los Angeles, which provides medical training to bring up-to-date health care services to inner cities all across America.

Elementary schools and junior high schools have been named for Charles Drew, too. In April of 1969, Lenore Drew attended the dedication of the Charles Drew Elementary School in Miami, Florida. Her husband "was a modest man," she told the students. "I'm sure that he would be amazed that a school building would be erected in his memory."

In 1976, a group of about 700 of Drew's friends, family members, and medical professionals gathered to honor Drew as a portrait of him was hung at the Clinical Center of the National Institutes of Health, in Washington, D.C. It is the first portrait of an African-American to hang in the center's gallery of scientists.

Speaking at this tribute was Dr. Jack White, the former student Drew sent off to the "far northland." Now serving as director of the Cancer Research Center at the Howard University Medical School, White remarked, "I consider it luck that I had the privilege of being one of his residents. I rank him first among noble Americans."

In 1977, the American Red Cross rededicated its headquarters in Washington, D.C., as The Charles R. Drew Blood Center. Three years later, the U.S. Postal Service issued a Charles Drew postage stamp as part of its "Great Americans" series.

In 1986, a granite marker was placed at the site of the automobile accident that claimed Drew's life. The memorial was unveiled on April 5 by his daughter,

IN MEMORY OF
CHARLES RICHARD DREW
1904 — 1950

CHARLES RICHARD DREW
1904 - 1950

Charlene Drew Jarvis. Charles Watts, one of Drew's former students, said at the ceremony, "The marker will say to all men that a great man lost his life here."

A bronze plaque on the marker recalls the many achievements of Drew's life. The inscription ends with his own words:

> There must always be the continuing strug-
> gle to make the increasing knowledge of the world
> bear some fruit in increased understanding and
> in the production of human happiness.

Today, Charles Drew is a legendary figure. And some legends about him are untrue.

Some accounts of his life have stated that he was the first scientist to test plasma for blood transfusions. But Drew himself admitted that he built on the work of his fellow blood researchers.

Some accounts of his death say that the hospital to which Drew was taken refused to give him a blood transfusion because it didn't have any "black" blood. But for years, Drs. Ford, Bullock, and Johnson, who were with Drew until the moment of his death, have disputed this rumor.

It is unnecessary to obscure the legacy of Charles Drew with myths. Drew's work in blood research has been responsible for saving countless lives. His efforts to strengthen the skills and broaden the opportunities of African-American doctors improved the quality of health care for all Americans.

Perhaps Drew's own words on the very nature and spirit of achievement give the best summary of his life:

In the individual accomplishments of each man lies the success or failure of the group as a whole. The success of the group as a whole is the basis for any tradition which we may create. In such tradition lies the sense of discipleship and the inspiration which serves as a guide for those who come after, so that each man's job is not just his job alone but a part of a greater job whose horizons we at present can only dimly imagine for they are beyond our view.

For Further Reading

Readers who want to know more about Charles Drew may want to begin with the full-length biography by Charles Wynes, *Charles Richard Drew: The Man and the Myth* (University of Illinois Press, 1988). Richard Hardwick has written *Charles Richard Drew: Pioneer in Blood Research* (Scribners, 1967), and Robert Lichello has covered Drew's life and career in *Pioneer in Blood Plasma: Dr. Charles Richard Drew* (Simon & Schuster, 1968).

Lenore Robbins Drew is the author of a personal profile of Charles Drew: "The Unforgettable Charlie Drew" (*Reader's Digest*, March 1978).

A chapter is devoted to Drew in *Blood Brothers: Four Men of Science*, by Emma Gleders Stone (Knopf, 1959). This history of blood-related research also has chapters on William Harvey, Marcello Malpighi, and Karl Landsteiner. Brief histories of blood research can be found in *How Did We Find Out About Blood?* by Isaac Asimov (Walker, 1986), and *The Circulatory System*, by Regina Avraham (Chelsea House, 1989).

Information on the American civil rights movement is available from many sources. A history of the struggle for racial equality from the early 1950s to the present is found in *Eyes on the Prize*, by Juan Williams (Viking, 1987). *The Civil Rights Movement in America*, by Patricia and Frederick McKissack (Childrens Press, 1991), covers the years from 1865 to the present.

Index

American Board of Surgery 7-10, 52, 64

American Medical Association 72-74

American Red Cross 11, 54, 56, 59, 63, 78-79

Amherst College 12, 22-32, 36, 49, 71, 78

Beattie, John 38-41, 55

blood
banking 10-11, 39-41, 44-48, 51-62, 78
plasma 38, 45-48, 54-63, 78, 81
research 10-11, 38-41, 43-48, 52, 54-58, 60, 64, 70, 72, 77-78, 81
transfusions 10, 38-39, 44-50, 54-55, 58, 62-64, 77-78, 81
type 38-39, 44, 46-48, 62

"Blood for Britain" 11, 54-60

Columbia-Presbyterian Medical Center 43-44, 51, 56

Columbia University Medical School 43-44, 64

Drew, Charlene Rosella 68, 79-81

Drew, Charles Richard
athletics 21-23, 25-31, 34-36
childhood 15-21
death 76-77
education 22-41
race relations 11-14, 16-18, 21, 25, 29-30, 32, 62-63, 72-74
research 10-11, 38-41, 43-48, 52, 54-58, 60, 70-72, 81

surgery 7-12, 21, 31, 41-44, 51-53, 64-68, 71-72, 78
teaching 7-12, 31, 42-43, 64-74, 77-78

Drew, Charles Richard, Jr. 68

Drew, Elsie 18, 30

Drew, Eva 18

Drew, Joseph 18, 21, 32

Drew, Lenore Robbins 7-9, 29, 49-53, 59, 62, 68-70, 75-77, 79

Drew, Nora (mother) 15, 18-19

Drew, Nora (sister) 18, 21

Drew, Rhea Sylvia 68

Drew, Richard 15, 18-19

Drew, Roberta ("Bebe") 53

Dunbar High School 22-23, 25

Freedmen's Bureau 41-42

Freedmen's Hospital 42, 53, 65, 71-73, 76

Howard University Medical School 7-10, 19, 32-33, 41-43, 48-50, 53-54, 59, 63, 65, 71-72, 77, 79

Johnson, Mordecai 9, 42, 77

Landsteiner, Karl 38-39, 44

McGill University Medical School 12, 33-41, 44, 55

McLaughry, "Tuss" 26, 29-30, 36

Montreal General Hospital 38-41

Scudder, John 44, 51-52, 54, 56, 64

World War II 10-12, 54-63, 78